M

By United Library

https://campsite.bio/unitedlibrary

Table of Contents

Disclaimer

This biography book is a work of nonfiction based on the public life of a famous person. The author has used publicly available information to create this work. While the author has thoroughly researched the subject and attempted to depict it accurately, it is not meant to be an exhaustive study of the subject. The views expressed in this book are those of the author alone and do not necessarily reflect those of any organization associated with the subject. This book should not be taken as an endorsement, legal advice, or any other form of professional advice. This book was written for entertainment purposes only.

Introduction

The book Moses reveals the enigmatic life and enduring legacy of the central figure revered in Judaism, Christianity, Islam and other Abrahamic religions. Considered the supreme prophet, Moses played a crucial role as leader of the Israelites and the revered lawgiver credited with writing the Torah.

Born in a time of oppression, Moses' journey unfolds from his miraculous rescue as an infant from Pharaoh's decree to kill Hebrew children to his adoption into the Egyptian royal family. Escaping after a fatal altercation, he meets the divine in the fiery ruin on Mount Horeb, setting the stage for his mission to lead the Israelites out of slavery.

The narrative runs through the Exodus, with Moses confronting Pharaoh and leading his people across the Red Sea to Mount Sinai, where he receives the Ten Commandments. The book delves into the complexities of Moses' character, his encounters with God and the challenges of leadership during his 40 years of wandering in the desert.

While the biblical Moses remains a subject of academic debate, this comprehensive exploration incorporates historical perspectives, examining references in ancient Egyptian literature and in the writings of historians such as Josephus Flavius. This book is a compelling journey through the life of an iconic and influential figure whose impact resonates across the millennia.

Moses

Moses was for Jews the quintessential *rav* (*Moshé Rabbenu*, Moses our teacher), and for both Jews and Christians he was the leader of the Jewish people according to the biblical account of the Exodus; for Muslims, however, Moses was first and foremost one of the prophets of Islam whose original revelation, however, was lost.

The biblical text explains the name "Moses," as a derivation from the root משה, connected to the semantic field of "drawing out of the water," in Exodus 2:10. It is suggested in this verse that the name is related to "drawing out of the water" in a passive sense; Moses would be "the one who was drawn out of the water." Others, distancing themselves from this tradition, derive the name from the same root, but with an active sense: "he who draws out," in the sense of "savior, deliverer" (in fact, in the Masoretic text the word is vocalized as an active participle, not a passive one). In the Egyptian language, Moses could mean *boy* or even *son* or *descendant*, as in the proper names *Thutmose* (*Dhwty-ms*), "son of Toth," or *Ramose* (*R-ms-sw*), "son of Ra."

According to tradition, Moses was born to the Israelites Amram and Iochebed, escaped persecution at Pharaoh's behest, was rescued by Pharaoh's daughter and educated in the Egyptian court. He fled from her following a murder committed against an overseer and retired to the land of Midian where he married Zipporah, daughter of the local priest. According to the Bible near Mount Horeb he received God's call and, upon returning to Egypt, confronted Pharaoh demanding the liberation of the people of Israel from slavery; Pharaoh would accept his proposal only following the ten plagues of Egypt, the last of which was the death of Egypt's firstborn sons. Encamped with his people near Yam Suf (Sea of Reeds), Moses, on divine instructions, parted the waters of the sea, thus enabling his people to cross it and finally submerging the Pharaonic army that had run after them. After a three-month journey, the prophet reached Mount Sinai where he received the Tablets of the Law and punished his people for worshiping a golden calf. Arriving near the promised land after 40 years of hard marching, Moses died on Mount Nebo before entering it.

He is considered a key figure in Judaism, Christianity, Islam, Bahaism, Rastafarianism, Mormonism, and many other religions. For Jews he is the greatest prophet who ever lived, for Christians the one who received the divine law, for Islamists one of the greatest predecessors of Muhammad. His story is told not only in the Holy Scriptures but also in the *Midrash*, *De Vita Mosis* by Philo of Alexandria, and the texts of Josephus Flavius. Moses is

venerated as a saint by the Catholic Church, which
commemorates him on September 4.

Description

Historical context

The figure of Moses and the biblical event of the Exodus do not, for scholars, possess any historical significance, but should be regarded as a religious narrative that integrates various elements even from different eras.

While some ancient authors-including Josephus Flavius and Herodotus, proponents of the *Ancient Exodus* theory-held to date the episodes of the Exodus with the expulsion of the hyksos, the Semitic pharaohs driven out of Egypt by Ahmose (ca. 1550-1525 BCE.), modern scholars tend to date the episode in the Egyptian New Kingdom, the expulsion of the hyksos being only a terminus *ante quem*, since this Indo-European people would have introduced the war chariot, later also used by the Pharaohs of the Egyptian New Kingdom, and particularly in the 13th century B.C, that is, straddling the reigns of Rameses II and his successor Merenptah. The Judaic epic connected with these events would have been put in writing, according to the most widely accepted theory of Torah formation, in the first period of the reign, 10th century BCE (Jahvist tradition), then reworked in the Northern Kingdom in the 8th century following the division of the kingdom (Elohist tradition), until reaching its final version in the 7th century BCE.C. by some priests in the southern kingdom (Deuteronomist tradition) in the era just before deportation, under the reign of Josiah, to emphasize their own religious characteristics.

Biblical sources

The books of the Pentateuch, also called the *books of Moses*, since according to the ancients written by him, have (except Genesis) the prophet as the main character:

- The Book of Exodus, from the Greek *exit*, recounts the oppression of the Israelite people, the subsequent persecution of the unborn wanted by Pharaoh, and the conception and salvation of the newborn Moses, raised by the ruler's daughter and becoming a prophet as a result of the divine call. It describes the confrontation with the new Pharaoh, the plagues of Egypt and the exodus across the sea, concluding with the Law on Mount Sinai and the various norms of community life.

- Leviticus does not narrate episodes from Moses' life, but Moses is nonetheless the protagonist of the book; to him God entrusts the rules regarding rituals, sacrifices and various ceremonies.

- The Book of Numbers picks up the thread of history interrupted by Leviticus, describing Israel's journey through the wilderness that separated it from the promised land, beginning at Mount Sinai and ending at the threshold of Canaan, after a 40-year sojourn in Kades.

- Deuteronomy presents three speeches by Moses, who, before his death, reminds the people of past events and takes up in new accents the Law already defined in Exodus. The book concludes with an account of Joshua's succession and the prophet's death on Mount Nebo.

- Various subsequent passages, particularly in the Psalms, remind the people of Israel of the prodigies that occurred in the time of Moses.

The biblical Moses

Name

According to biblical texts, the name Moses would mean *rescued from the waters* in memory of his miraculous finding in the Nile and indeed the Hebrew *Moses* has an assonance with the verb meaning to *draw out*, although to this day most scholars prefer to believe that the name derives from the Egyptian root *Moses*, meaning *son of* or *begotten from* as we can for example see in the Egyptians Thutmosis (son of Thot) or Rameses (son of Ra). In line with this thesis and lacking the father's name Moses simply means *child* as a vein for *son*.

- The classical interpretation of the Midrash identifies Moses as one of seven biblical characters called by different names. Moses' other names were in fact: Jekuthiel (for his mother), Heber (for his father), Jered (for Miriam), Avi Zanoah (for Aaron), Avi Soco (for his wet nurse), Shemaiah ben Nethanel (for the people of Israel). Moses is also given the names Toviah (as a first name) and Levi (as a family name), Mechoqeiq (as a lawgiver) and Ehl Gav Ish.

- The Egyptian name *Moses* meaning, as already mentioned, *son* or *protégé of was* given to the prophet by Pharaoh's daughter when he was found by her on the banks of the river. The name then took on the meaning of *draw out* only later, when Moses delivered the people across the waters of the Red Sea. Josephus Flavius also mentions this etymology.

- Some Jewish scholars in the Middle Ages speculated that Moses' name was actually translated by the Bible authors from an Egyptian term meaning to *draw out*.

- According to Islamic tradition, his name, Mūsā, is said to be derived from two Egyptian words: *mu* meaning water and *sha* meaning reed or tree, due to the fact that his basket got stuck among the reeds at Pharaoh's house.

Family ties

Of the tribe of Levi, Moses was the son of Amram and his aunt Yochebed, both of the same household; Yochebed married his nephew-being the daughter of Levi, Jacob's son-although this narrative creates an anachronism concerning Moses, who should thus have been born some 40 years after the Hebrews arrived in Egypt. Moses' siblings were Aaron, three years older, and Miriam (or Mary) whose age we ignore, although we know she is the eldest, having followed her unborn brother when he was abandoned by his mother along the banks of the Nile.

In Midian, Moses married Zipporah (or Sefora), daughter of the priest Jethro, by whom he had two sons, Gershon (whose name means *immigrant* since he was born in a foreign land) and Eliezer. The book of Numbers mentions an Ethiopian wife of Moses, whom some exegetes assume to be Zipporah herself, referring the Hebrew term Kushite (i.e., Ethiopian) also to a Midian tribe, while other exegetes disagree, believing them to be two different characters, also in view of the various traditions woven about Moses' family and detailed below. Josephus Flavius, heir to the Hebrew tradition, narrates in this regard the episode of the war of Moses, still an Egyptian captain, in Ethiopia where he married Tharbis, sister of the enemy king, thus stipulating peace with him.

The analysis of Moses' family ties highlights difficulties, given the intertwining of several contradictory biblical traditions; note the scholars of the École biblique et archéologique française (the editors of the Jerusalem Bible) that "the texts do not agree on the name and person of Moses' father-in-law. We have here [Ex2:18] Reuèl, priest of Midian; in 3:1; 4:18; 18:1 he is called Jethro; Nm10:29 speaks of Obab, son of Reuèl, the Midianite; Jdc1:16; 4:11 of Obab the Kenite. [...] In fact the two traditions about a Kenite marriage and a

Midianite marriage are competitors and one should not try to reconcile them. The first, originating in southern Palestine, reflects the existence of friendly ties between Judah and the Kenites, preserving the memory of Moses' marriage to a foreigner. The second is more closely related to the exit from Egypt," and even TOB interdenominational Bible scholars believe that "different traditions give Moses' father-in-law different names, without trying to harmonize them."

Socio-cultural training

Moses, adopted by Pharaoh's daughter, joined the court, where he was no doubt educated in the wisdom of the Egyptians, as Stephen also records in the Acts of the Apostles. The prophet was thus familiar in detail with the future enemy, its customs and traditions; Exodus also tells us that he was a man highly esteemed in Egypt "in the eyes of the ministers, Pharaoh and the people." And in this connection we might recall the aforementioned episode of the Ethiopian War, in which Moses distinguished himself as an able and valiant general.

Having escaped to Midian, he learned about the customs of the desert peoples, the caravan routes and, according to some, searching for drinking water, even a series of phenomena that made it possible to cross the waters of the Red Sea while remaining unharmed.

Psychological traits

Very complex: powerful and restless, tame and noble, between the legendary and the real. Mircea Eliade will say, "His biography and personality traits completely elude us. By the mere fact that he became a charismatic and legendary figure, his life conforms to the pattern of so many heroes."

Moses is presented from the earliest chapters as a courageous man, determined to defend the weakest: he first confronts an Egyptian overseer to save a slave, and then a group of shepherds chasing some maidens from a well. Although presented as a heroic figure, Moses does not escape moments of fear, covering his face before the burning bush "because he was afraid," fleeing when the staff turns into a serpent, even trying to avoid returning to Egypt and meeting Pharaoh because he was "clumsy of mouth and tongue," rejecting the divine proposal and even saying "Forgive me my Lord, send whom you will!"

Back in Egypt, however, Moses shows great courage in Pharaoh's court, openly defying the ruler and raging at him because of his obstinacy. The prophet instills courage in the Israelites during the Red Sea crossing and during the wilderness wanderings, acting as a spokesman between man and God, asking the latter for food and water for his people. He is a *meek* man, patient with his people, though not exempt from strong moments of anger, as when he punished the Israelites following the worship of the golden calf.

He is presented in the Bible as an exemplary leader, stern with a *hard-hearted* people, ready to punish and forgive, a figure who remained engraved in the hearts of the Israelites because of his special charisma so much so that they after centuries still remembered him as a man of extraordinary ability *no prophet like Moses has arisen in Israel since*.

Biography

Birth and youth

Born to Yochebed and Amram, baby Moses was hidden in a basket by his mother when he was only three months old and laid on the banks of the Nile to be saved from the persecution Pharaoh wanted. For Pharaoh had said to his people, "Behold, the people of the children of Israel are more numerous and stronger than we are. Let us take measures against it to prevent it from increasing, otherwise, in case of war, it will join our adversaries, fight against us and then depart from the land." He then imposed forced labor on the Jews to oppress them. But the Hebrew people continued to increase so the king of Egypt told the midwives of the Hebrews to kill the Hebrews' male children, but the midwives did not. Then Pharaoh gave this order to all his people, "Every male child that is born to the Hebrews, you shall cast into the Nile, but you shall let every daughter live." From the waters of the Nile, Moses was picked up by the ruler's daughter who, moved by the baby's crying, decided to adopt him as her son, entrusting him, at the invitation of Miriam, the infant's sister, to his birth mother to nurture.

The subject of Moses' birth, even according to Christian scholars, ranks among the "childhood narratives of famous men," both real and mythological, that is, "stories of birth and youth that were shaped in retrospect after the subjects had become famous." The TOB Bible highlights in this regard, "the epic that was told in the East around Sargon of Akkad, a great Mesopotamian conqueror of the 25th century B.C.," who was also secretly given birth by his mother and abandoned in the river in a basket of reeds, further pointing out how "this tale was still recopied in Egypt shortly before the time of the Exodus. If it was able to serve as a framework for the tradition concerning Moses, it is because they wanted to put the liberator of Israel on the level of the great figures of history." Concordantly, the "New Great Biblical Commentary" also recalls the epic of Sargon of Akkad and also points out another narrative predating the Mosaic one: "an Egyptian myth says that the goddess Isis hid her newborn son Horus in a papyrus bush in the delta to save him from death threatened by Seth"; Rudolf Bultmann also believes there are older, common traditions behind the narratives of the slaughter of the Hebrew firstborn in the story of Moses and the slaughter of the innocents commanded by Herod after the birth of Jesus.

Brought up in the Egyptian court and educated in its culture (as would later happen to Daniel at Nebuchadnezzar in Babylon) Moses went one day to the Israelites' yard where, defending a slave, he killed the overseer who was beating him without being seen but, having hidden his body in the sand, he discovered that the murder was common knowledge when he tried to stop a quarrel between two slaves. Wanted by Pharaoh he abandoned Egypt and fled, across the desert, to the land of Midian.

Exile in Midian

Stopping by a well, Moses met the seven daughters of Jethro, priest of Midian, and defended them from the assault of some overbearing shepherds. The young women, grateful to their defender, introduced him to their father, who invited him to stay with them. In Midian, Moses became a shepherd in the priest's service and married one of his daughters, Sefora (or Zipporah), by whom he had two boys, Gershon and Eliezer.

While leading the flocks to the pastures of Mount Horeb, Moses was attracted by the marvelous wonder of a bush that burned but was not consumed; from it came a voice ordering him to remove his sandals because he was treading on holy ground, later revealing himself as the God of the patriarchs of Israel who, having heard the cry of the slaves, had decided to free them and lead them to a land "where flows milk and honey." Moses, having been ordered to be leader of the Israelites, first refused the assignment out of fear, wondering what God's name was and how he could convince his people that he himself had sent him to redeem them.

"I am who I am" was the answer coming from the bush, which also indicated to the prophet the signs to be given to the Israelites: his staff turned into a snake, his hand became leprous, and water turned into blood. Tormented by anguish, Moses replied that he was unable to speak in Pharaoh's presence because he was clumsy; God therefore declared to place his brother Aaron beside him so that he could assist him and speak for him in times of trouble.

Returning from Jethro, Moses narrated what had happened and asked permission to leave with his wife and son for Egypt, while according to another tradition he left instead alone. A curious incident, however, disturbed his journey: "in the place where he stayed overnight" he was struck by an evil that put his life in danger, a sign of a heavenly sanction. The reason that emerges is the fact that he had delayed, for his son and perhaps also for himself, the rite of circumcision, the physical sign of the Covenant entered into by God with Abraham's seed. Perhaps Moses, having become the son-in-law of the Midianite priest, had merely conformed to the Midianite custom according to which, as with other neighboring peoples, this practice served as an initiation rite marking the entrance to marriageable age and was thus reserved for young men who had reached the threshold of adulthood and not for eight-day-old infants.The inclusion of this unclear affair in the narrative certainly invokes strict adherence to the customs in use in Israel at the time of the final redaction of the sacred text, operated in priestly circles and later scrupulously adopted. The threat immediately recedes as soon as order is restored: it was Zipporah herself who performed the ritual operation on Gershon and later placed her son's foreskin on Moses' penis, simulating circumcision to save him from divine wrath.

The ancient proscript thus returned to Egypt. Aaron inspired to this end, went to meet him in the desert and received his divine instructions pertaining to his role as coadjutor.

Return to Egypt

Having assembled the elders of Israel, Moses showed them the wonders of the Lord and communicated his intention to go to Pharaoh to ask for the deliverance of his own people. Going with his brother into the presence of the ruler, he asked permission to retire to the desert for three days with the slaves so as to sacrifice to their God and honor him. Pharaoh, in response to their requests, ordered his overseers to duplicate the work of the Israelites by having them gather straw to make bricks, which until recently had been granted to them by the Egyptians themselves.

Oppressed by the greater burden, the Israelites could not get the job done, so their scribes were flogged and beaten; having received the punishment and not having obtained from Pharaoh the grace of a rebate, they bitterly rebuked Moses and Aaron who had caused all this.

The Levites, at the divine invitation, again went to court, showing in the presence of Pharaoh and his ministers the prodigy of the staff turned into a serpent. The latter, little astonished by the event, ordered his magicians to do likewise, and so it happened, except that the Israelites' staff devoured that of the Egyptian sorcerers.

Deliverer of the people of Israel

Moses went to Pharaoh again while it was still morning and Pharaoh was relaxing by the Nile River. Moses asked for the release of his people, but God had "hardened Pharaoh's heart"-so that Pharaoh would persist in not letting the Israelites leave and thus be able to strike Egypt with plagues-and the ruler refused; then Aaron struck the waters of the river with his own staff, which turned to blood: fish died, and the Nile became so fetid that the Egyptians could no longer draw water from it. Pharaoh's magicians, however, managed to perform the same prodigy, and the ruler returned to his palace without heeding Moses. The Egyptians dug wells around the Nile to draw water to drink; the drought lasted seven days.

Aaron therefore struck the rivers, canals and ponds of Egypt with his own staff, and frogs began to come out of them in infinite numbers, pouring over the houses of Pharaoh and his subjects. The magicians succeeded in performing the same prodigy. The frightened ruler asked Moses to make such a plague stop but as soon as it was averted he persisted and did not heed the prophet's words.

At the Lord's command, Aaron beat the dust and it turned into mosquitoes that infested the whole land of Egypt. The magicians failed this time and they themselves asked Pharaoh for mercy as they recognized in those prodigies the hand of God. However, the ruler, whose heart continued to be "hardened" by the Lord, remained firm in his convictions. The Lord then sent against the Egyptians a host of flies that invaded their dwellings. Pharaoh, terrified by this event, asked Moses and Aaron for forgiveness and ordered them to sacrifice in honor of God. The two, however, refused because during their celebrations some animals sacred to the Egyptians would be killed. Pharaoh allowed them to leave Egypt for three days. As soon as the flies disappeared, the tyrant ordered his soldiers to lead the Israelites back into slavery.

Faced with this umpteenth rejection, a plague killed all the livestock of the Egyptians. The Israelites' livestock, however, survived. Aaron and Moses returned to Pharaoh carrying furnace soot in their hands. Before the eyes of the ruler they threw it into the air and it produced purulent ulcers on the Egyptians and their livestock. The magicians this time could not even appear before Pharaoh.

Hail poured down on Egypt, uprooting trees and plants, striking the Egyptians and their livestock. Again Pharaoh repented for his behavior but, as soon as the plague was averted, he continued to beat the Israelite slaves. The flax and barley had been destroyed by hail but the wheat and spelt were still intact.

Moses and Aaron went to Pharaoh again, but Pharaoh would not listen to them. They then revealed the Lord's orders: he would send, with a strong east wind, a host of locusts that would devour what the hail had not destroyed. The frightened Pharaoh ordered them to leave, but leaving the women and children in Egypt, but Moses did not consent and was therefore driven out of the royal palace. The next day the locusts destroyed every crop.

Moses therefore stretched out his staff toward the sky, and for three days the land of Egypt was darkened and the darkness was so thick that no one could move. Pharaoh summoned Moses and Aaron and ordered them to depart, but left their livestock in Egypt. The two prophets did not consent, and the ruler, whose heart was once again "hardened" by the Lord, drove Moses away, threatening to kill him.

Finally, the Lord commanded the two Levites to prepare for a long journey as He would send a final plague that would force Pharaoh to release them. He also commanded them to commemorate that day for centuries to come through the festival of Pesach

As soon as the angel of death descended on the land of Egypt and saw that lamb's blood, he would pass on, recognizing in it an Israelite home. The Jews gathered in their homes to celebrate the feast of deliverance. On their tables were lamb meat, unleavened *haste* bread, and bitter herbs, symbolizing the suffering of slavery. While these dined, at midnight the plague came upon the Egyptians. Every firstborn died, from Pharaoh's firstborn to the firstborn of every one of his servants. The ruler, grieved by the death of his son, ordered the Hebrews to leave and, to hasten their departure, supplied them with gold and silver.

Leaving Pi-Rameses, the Israelites took Joseph's remains with them so that they could rest in the promised land as the patriarch had been promised before his death. Moses, on divine instructions, decided not to take the shortest route, called the *Philistines'* route, because it was equipped with Egyptian forts. He continued on by the desert route, toward the Sea of Reeds (traditionally and perhaps erroneously identified with the Red Sea). According to the book of Exodus, God led his people, by day as a pillar of cloud, by night as a pillar of fire, to light their passage.

Pharaoh meanwhile regretted letting the Israelites leave, and so did his ministers. He therefore had his own chariot prepared, armed himself and gathered his soldiers. He took six hundred war chariots from among the best with the third man on top of each and reached the Israelites while they were encamped by the sea. The prophet, encouraging his people, asked the Lord for help, and at that same instant the pillar of fire, which was leading the Israelites, came between them and the Egyptians, thus stopping the latter's charge.

Moses therefore stretched out his staff over the sea and, in what is perhaps among the most famous legendary accounts in the Bible, the waters parted, thus forming a wall to the right and left, with the dry in the middle. The Israelites were thus able to cross the sea and reach the other shore, while the Egyptians pursued them in their chariots, ending up submerged when they were safe. There were no survivors among the Egyptians. According to Islamic tradition, Pharaoh, before the waters submerged him, told Moses that he believed God, but he was not saved because the words were not sincere.

From the Red Sea to Mount Sinai

Near the desert of Sur, after a three-day journey, Moses ordered them to camp near the locality of Mara having run out of water supplies; there, however, it was not possible to draw water as it was bitter to drink. Moses, on divine command, threw a miraculous shrub on the surface of the lake that made its waters drinkable.

The people, already tired from the hard journey, complained to Moses since they had run out of food supplies as well. The Lord, pitying the Israelites, commanded the prophet to announce that they would soon find something to feed themselves. That very evening a flock of quail, driven there by a strong wind, stopped by the camp, becoming easy prey for the Israelites, who the next morning, instead, found scattered around the camp small grains of a strange resinous substance, tasting like *honeyed flatbread*. Moses named that food, Man hu, meaning *what is it?* He also ordered the Israelites to gather it in jugs, each family according to its need; each day they would gather that food, only on the sixth day were they to take twice as much since the Sabbath was a day of rest and work was forbidden. Those who, having feared that they would not receive what was promised, gathered more food than was necessary to feed themselves for one day, found worms in it.

Likewise...as soon as the water supply was finished, the Lord commanded Moses in the locality of Refidim to go to a mountain and command the rock to gush out. Moses, however, struck the rock twice with his staff. As soon as the rock was struck by the prophet's rod, all the water needed for the Israelites gushed out of it.That place was named Massa and Meriba which means *test* and *protest..*

While still encamped there, the Israelites were attacked by the Amalekites, a Bedouin population from the southern part of Canaan. Moses therefore instructed Joshua, his future successor, to organize the defense while he would climb to a nearby high ground with Aaron and Korah to watch the fighting from above. Whenever Moses prayed, raising his arms and holding his staff pointed toward heaven, Israel won while when he lowered it, he lost. The fighting was prolonged and the prophet was barely able and with the help of Aaron and Kur to keep his arms up, thus enabling Joshua to win the battle and defeat the Amalekites.

The Israelites finally arrived, after three months of walking, at the foot of Mount Sinai where they camped. In those days Jethro, Moses' father-in-law, set out to join him. Among the activities that Moses carried out on a daily basis, the most demanding was undoubtedly that of judge and counselor; he sat among the people, and anyone who had questions to ask would turn to him, who judged disputes and listened to the problems of his own people. This activity, however, was very tiring; Jethro quickly realized that one person alone could not handle such a heavy task for long, and he advised his son-in-law to choose wise and honest men and place them at the head of groups of a hundred, ten, a thousand people, so the people would quickly find someone to consult with in their time of need and Moses would have more time to deal with more important matters.

The legislature

On divine command Moses went up to the slopes of Mount Sinai and was ordered to prepare the people since the Lord wanted to show himself to them and communicate his will. After three days of purification, the Israelites saw thunder and lightning descending on the mountain, which became *like a furnace* frightened they retreated and it was only Moses who advanced and received by the mouth of God the law of the Ten Commandments:

Terrified, the Israelites begged Moses to go up toward the mountain since they were afraid of dying from fear. The prophet obeyed and entered the cloud, climbing the slopes of Sinai, where he remained for forty days and forty nights, accompanied only by Joshua, his faithful associate, who followed him from afar. There he received the law, written on two stone tablets by the *finger of God*, or, according to another biblical tradition, written by Moses himself.

Downstream meanwhile, the people of Israel, believing that Moses was dead, implored Aaron, who had taken over in his brother's absence, to build an idol for them so that it would guide them to the Promised Land. A golden calf was thus forged to which the Israelites sacrificed and around which they reveled. When he came down from the mountain the prophet was inflamed with wrath, destroyed the idol and bitterly rebuked Aaron who *had taken all restraint from them,* then ordered those who remained faithful to him to kill all who rebelled. According to the book of Exodus about three thousand men fell that day.

From Sinai to the Paran Desert

Following the prescriptions he received at Sinai, Moses summoned the leading artists of the people of Israel and ordered them to build a tent, called the *Abode*, in which to keep the tablets of the law, laid in the famous *ark of the covenant*, and to be able to perform sacrifices and ritual practices at the hands of the priesthood, headed by Aaron and his sons, as well as the entire tribe of Levi, who were charged with the supervision and care of the Abode.

After two years spent on the slopes of Sinai, Moses, having completed the census of all the people, led the

Israelites across the desert to the land of Canaan. After a three-day march he made them camp near the town of Taberah, where a severe fire decimated the Israelites, who rebelled against their leader. The latter despondently retreated to the Dwelling Place, and praying to God asked to die so as not to listen to the lament of his people, who now accused him of letting them starve, filled with manna but deprived of meat. At divine command, Moses chose seventy elders of Israel to support him in his arduous task. By evening the camp was again overrun with quails, so numerous that they "came out of their nostrils and came to them in boredom." The greediest were killed by a mysterious evil, a sign of divine wrath.

That issue resolved, Moses had to face a new rebellion this time organized by members of his own family-Miriam and Aaron. Both challenged their brother's authority, believing themselves to be prophets like him and accusing him of having a wife foreign to the people of Israel. Punished for her rebellion, Miriam became leprous and had to flee the camp for about a week, as was required by the ritual laws.

Having healed her of her illness, Moses resumed his journey and camped with his people in the wilderness of Paran, near the promised land. From there he sent out twelve men, representing each tribe, to scout. Among them was Joshua, Moses' future successor. The latter, upon his return, was the only one, along with Caleb, another scout, who thought the promised land conquerable, unlike his companions who thought it impenetrable, thus causing a rebellion against Moses to return to Egypt. The prophet narrowly succeeded in appeasing the divine wrath, which was intended to destroy the entire people, who were nevertheless punished with the decree that they could not enter the promised land until 40 years had passed, so that the generation that had rebelled would die and their descendants would enter it as free men.

The forty years spent in the desert

Pursued and killed by the inhabitants of Canaan, the Israelites took refuge in the wilderness where Core, Dathan and Abiram, at the head of 200 men, rose up against Moses and Aaron, accusing them of wanting to place themselves above other members of the community. They especially opposed Aaron's priestly investiture because, according to the three conspiratorial leaders, all the people of Israel were holy.

To settle the matter, Moses ordered them to present themselves, accompanied by their incense burners, before the Dwelling Place. When everyone was there, Moses challenged them to offer incense as a sacrifice, a ritual action reserved exclusively for Aaron and his sons.

In the presence of the people of Israel, Aaron's staff miraculously flourished, a sign that God approved his election to the priesthood, rejecting that of the conspirators, whose censers were melted down and used to cover the altar of sacrifice.

Upon reaching Kades, the Israelites paid funeral honors to Miriam, who was buried there. There the people also complained to Moses and Aaron about the lack of water. The two prophets went to the Dwelling Place and asked the Lord for advice, being instructed by him, to strike a rock with their staff, as they had already done at Refidim. Moses and Aaron did as they had been instructed but no water initially came out of the rock. Intimidated by this failure they repeated the action and succeeded. Having doubted God they were both punished: they would never set foot in the promised land.

After 38 years of long waiting, the Israelites set out again and, having to pass through the borders of the kingdom of Edom, asked the local ruler to let them pass. The latter did not agree and sent his men to exterminate them, thus forcing Moses and his men to flee and settle momentarily on the slopes of Mount Cor. There Moses stripped Aaron of his priestly garments since, being close to death, he would, according to ritual, defile them, after which he appointed his nephew Eleazar, Aaron's son, as the new high priest. The latter died at the top of the mountain and was buried there.

After a fierce battle with the Canaanite king Arad, who was defeated with all his troops, the Israelites rebelled again against Moses and were therefore invaded by a host of poisonous snakes that attacked the conspirators, killing them. The people repented for their behavior and asked forgiveness from Moses, who, at divine invitation, constructed a bronze snake, put it on a pole, and all who looked upon it were healed.

Having dismantled the camp, the Israelites were attacked by the king of the Amorites, Sicon, who ended up defeated and killed, as did later the giant Og, king of Bashan: their cities were destroyed and the territories conquered. Saved from war with the king of Moab, Balak, the Israelites camped near his kingdom and there were lured by the local women who drove them to idolatry. Moses ordered them to be punished at once, and Pincas - Aaron's nephew - killed, by piercing them in the lower abdomen with a spear, a couple consisting of a Midianite and a Hebrew, and by that act obtained the everlasting priesthood for Aaron's lineage; the Lord then stopped the scourge, which had led to the death of 24,000 Israelites. These events led to the war and extermination of the Midianites, although this event is not considered historical; according to the biblical narrative, the Israelites slaughtered all the Midianites but spared the women and children, and this infuriated Moses, who ordered them all to be killed, keeping only the virgin maidens as booty.

The time having come to enter the Promised Land, Moses appointed Joshua as his successor and before leaving his people forever, the prophet gave them his testament, three dialogues contained in the book of Deuteronomy. In the first discourse the stages of the wilderness journey are summarized with the admonition to keep God's law if one does not want to lose the Land gained after this arduous journey, and in the second discourse we have in fact a heartfelt reminder of the observance of this law itself and the accompanying penalties. After blessing the tribes of Israel Moses went up, from the steppes of Moab, to Mount Nebo and from up there he could look down on the Promised Land, without being able to enter it because of his lack of it at the waters of Meribah.

In conclusion, Moses' life, according to the biblical narrative, can be divided into exactly three periods of 40 years each: the first 40 as an Egyptian as the adopted son of the daughter of the then ruling Pharaoh. When, in order to save and defend an Israelite, he killed an Egyptian, he fled to the desert, as the news soon became public knowledge. The next 40 years he spent with his father-in-law Jethro in the land of Midian as a shepherd, where he was able to meditate and learn humility so that he would be ready to lead his people out of Egypt. The last 40, he spent wandering in the desert to the promised land, Canaan. He died at the age of 120.

Apocrypha and later legends

Pharaoh's crown

According to an ancient legend, also reported by Josephus Flavius, when Moses was only three years old, Pharaoh for fun took his own crown and placed it on the child's head. The latter threw it to the ground and stepped on it, thus upsetting the ruler who asked his ministers whether this gesture was worthy of capital punishment.

The angel Gabriel, in the form of one of the wise men of the court, advised them to have precious stones and hot coals brought in and then let the child choose what to take. In this way they would be able to judge whether he had acted on purpose. Guided by the angel, Moses took the coal and brought it to his mouth, being injured on his lips and tongue.

It is speculated that this episode is only meant to provide an explanation for the speech defect from which Moses suffered.

The war against Kush

Taking up the narrative of Josephus Flavius, Pharaoh, seeing Moses grow into a strong and robust young man, decided to give him a war mission to test his temperament. He ordered his adopted grandson to fight south of Egypt against the kingdom of Kush (the Semitic name for present-day Ethiopia).

The opposing city had been fortified so as to be impregnable: very high walls on two sides, a deep canal with crocodiles on the third side, a moat filled with snakes on the fourth. Moses ordered some ibis to be captured and trained, with the help of which he was able to eliminate the snakes and thus approach the city walls unarmed.

The enemy generals saw him coming with a symbol of peace in his hand and, though frightened of a possible attack, let him in. Moses negotiated an honorable surrender with them, and all those who guaranteed peace and alliance for the future were allowed to keep their leadership roles, while those who fomented war and rebellion were removed.

Great were the festivities, during which, to seal the covenant, Moses had to marry the king's sister, Tharbis. This last reference served only to justify the discontent aroused by Aaron and Miriam over the presence of Moses' Ethiopian wife.

Assumption into heaven

According to a legend reported by Josephus Flavius, Moses was assumed into heaven at the end of his life. After ascending Mount Nebo and embracing Eleazar and Joshua, while he was talking to them a cloud suddenly descended over him and he disappeared. It was reported in the Pentateuch that he died a natural death, lest people think that he had ascended to God because of his extraordinary virtue.

Historicity

The issue of the historicity of Moses and the events narrated in Exodus is one that has been widely debated in academic circles. Those who have defended the historicity of the character in the past are countered by those who now see Moses as a figure with mythical or legendary contours, while keeping in mind that "a Moses-like figure may have existed somewhere in southern Transjordan in the second half of the 13th century B.C." and that archaeology is unable to confirm this.

Egyptologist Jan Assmann argues that it is not possible to know whether Moses ever lived because there are no traces of him outside the tradition. Although the names of Moses and others in the biblical narratives are Egyptian and the Book of Exodus contains genuine Egyptian elements, no extrabiblical source clearly points to Moses. No reference to Moses appears in any Egyptian source before the fourth century B.C., long after the period in which he is believed to have lived. No contemporary Egyptian source mentions Moses or the events narrated in the Pentateuch, nor has any archaeological evidence been discovered in Egypt or the Sinai desert to support the story in which he is the central figure.

David Adams Leeming considers Moses a mythical hero and the central figure of Hebrew mythology. Historian John van Seters believes that a historical Moses may have existed, but points out that "in the Pentateuch history becomes memory, which magnifies it and turns it into myth," concluding that "the search for the historical Moses is a futile endeavor: he now belongs only to legend."

The story of Moses' discovery by Pharaoh's daughter relates to a familiar theme in Near Eastern mythology, namely that of the leader of humble origins ascending to power. For example, Sargon of Akkad thus describes his origins:

My mother, the great priestess, conceived; in secret she carried me.

He put me in a basket of rushes, with bitumen he sealed the lid.

He threw me into the river that rose over me.

Some scholars, including Israel Finkelstein, while denying the historical truth of the relevant biblical narrative, regard it as the mythologizing of a confrontation pertaining to a lower chronology (from the 10th century B.C. onward) of Israel's history, such as the invasion of Israel by Pharaoh Sheshonq I after the death of King Solomon and the clash between King Josiah and Pharaoh

Necao II, thus believing that its protagonists are but the resultant sprung from what could be called *pious tradition.*

Most scholars, including Christian scholars, believe that the events recounted in the Bible regarding the Jewish presence in Egypt are not historical and therefore are not mentioned in the Egyptian documents of the time; in fact, even two extraordinary events - such as the escape of some three million slaves and the annihilation of the entire Egyptian army, including its cavalry - should have been reported not only in Egyptian documents but also in those of foreign rulers, who would have welcomed such news, given the possibility of invading such a fertile and rich land as Egypt; this did not happen and, indeed, extrabiblical historical sources attest that, during the reign of Rameses II and then his son and successor Merenptah, Egypt continued to have a powerful army and to be a dominant nation.

Historical Moses according to Sigmund Freud

Moses and Aton

According to Sigmund Freud, the biblical story of Moses would highlight the strong influence of the monotheistic culture and religion of the ancient Egyptian god Aton on ancient Jewish culture and its monotheism.

First of all, according to Freud, it should be noted that in the ancient Egyptian language, "Moses" had the meaning of "child," "son," "descendant," (see, for example, J. Lehmann, *Moses the Egyptian*). Moreover, the biblical account of Moses' birth, consistent with other Semitic legends, exactly echoes the birth account of the great Sargon of Accad, who was abandoned in the waters and then rescued to later become a great king.

We quote below what Freud says again about the origin of the well-known creed found in the Old Testament: *The Hebrew creed, as it is known, reads "Shemà Israel Adonai Elohenu Adonai Ehad." If the similarity of the Egyptian*

Aton's name to the Hebrew word Adonai and the Syriac divine name Adonis is not accidental, but comes from an old-fashioned unity of language and meaning, then the Hebrew formula could be translated thus, "Hear Israel our God Aton (Adonai) is the only God."

Also, again for Freud, the strong resemblance of Ps104, which sings the glory of God in creation, to the *Hymn to the Sun* of Akhenaten, the pharaoh who introduced the monotheistic worship of the god Aton in the 14th century B.C., should be noted.

The alleged relationship between the cult of Aton and Moses could be explained in two ways: while the case that Jews in Egypt followed such a cult is to be ruled out, there would remain the education that Moses received in the court of Pharaoh Haremhab, under whose reign Moses may have been born. Unspecified historical concurrences suggest that behind the *daughter of pharaoh* who adopted Moses was a noblewoman initiated into the cult of Aton, perhaps Queen Ankhesenamon, daughter of Akhenaten who ended up after various vicissitudes in marriage to Haremhab. While the most certain hypothesis is that Moses was a courtier of Akhenaten, and thus was certainly a follower of the cult of Aton; this hypothesis is supported by Moses' date of birth according to tradition on 7 Adar 2368 (corresponding to the years between 1391-1386 B.C.)

which makes him a contemporary of Pharaoh Akhenaten who lived in the 14th century B.C.

The theory of the *killing of Moses*

According to the famous father of psychoanalysis, Moses was not actually one man who freed the Israelites and led them to the Promised Land, but two different people.

The *first Moses*, the one who freed the Hebrews from Egypt, was an Egyptian, a fanatic of the monotheistic religion founded by Akhenaten, a follower, therefore, of Aton, the merciful god, who decided to set out to a land where his beliefs were not persecuted, as was the case in Egypt, taking with him the Semitic people and some Egyptian followers. These, while traveling in the desert, killed their teacher, and thus the first Moses.

Power therefore passed into the hands of a *second Moses*, a Midianite priest, faithful to a religion worshiping a volcanic and bloodthirsty God, who did not hesitate in asking his acolytes to pass "by the *edge of the sword*" all the inhabitants of the land of Canaan. This Midianite was none other than Jethro, the father-in-law of Moses, who, while traveling in the Sinai desert, visited his son-in-law and, after conversing with him in the tent (the place where, according to several followers of Freud's theory, the murder of the first Moses took place) went out, alone, and attended a banquet in the company of Aaron and the elders of Israel.

Moses the Egyptian

Sigmund Freud, in his book *Moses and Monotheism*, highlights these points:

1. Moses preaches in Egypt, like Akhenaten 50 or 100 years earlier, a monotheistic theology;

2. Moses has an Egyptian name;

3. Moses has, in the biblical account, an absolutely legendary birth;

4. a name of the Hebrew god (Adonai), has the same root as the solar god (Aton) of Amenhotep IV;

5. the Jewish ark of the covenant bears strong similarities to the "boat of the gods" of Egyptian temples, surrounded by cherubim with outstretched wings.

Josephus Flavius likens the figure of Moses to that of Hosarseph, a semi-legitimate figure in ancient Egyptian history, and says he refers to the writings of the anti-Semitic Egyptian astrologer and historian Manetho (Ptolemaic period, 4th or 3rd century B.C.), and counterarguments by the Greek Jewish historian Artapanus of Alexandria, both of whom discuss Moses as a single personality who historically existed between Israel and Egypt.

According to the Egyptian historian (again in the version of Josephus Flavius) Hosarseph was a high priest (perhaps First Prophet) of the clergy of Osiris from the city of Heliopolis who allegedly built a powerful following among the untouchables (a name perhaps indicating lepers) and was exiled, along with his followers, to the land of Canaan following a prophetic dream of the ruler. In the land of exile he would then organize, allying with the local peoples, a revolt that would lead him to conquer Egypt itself, exiling in turn, in Ethiopia, the ruler and his son Rapsaces, whose name is also said to be Sethos.After a thirteen-year reign marked by religious oppression Amenophis and his son would drive out the usurper by restoring the worship of the ancient gods.

A correct historical framing is difficult since there were as many as four rulers, all belonging to the 18th Egyptian dynasty, who bore the name Amenhotep, the original form of the *Greekised* Amenophis. Of the four Amenhoteps the one who could be most closely related to the ruler described by Manetho is Amenhotep III (1387 B.C. - 1348 B.C.) father of Akhenaten.

Moses in the three monotheistic religions

Jewish tradition

Jewish tradition, which has Moses as its highest representative, having received the tablets of the Law on Mount Sinai, has created around this figure a series of legends and myths that have expanded his epic depth: a child prodigy, he lit up his parents' room when he was conceived, at one year old he was already able to speak and at three he could predict the future. He became an Egyptian and maintained the customs of the Israelites and was miraculously saved from death when, captured by Pharaoh's soldiers, he was condemned to be beheaded but his neck was not even nicked by the executioner's sword, which fell shattered. He became the leader of his people and had to fight against the greed of the other Israelites, who wanted to grab the treasures of the Egyptians at all costs, and ascending Mount Sinai, he became, upon the teaching of the angels, master of the Torah, to him were communicated the wisdom writings of the Jewish tradition: the Talmud, the Mishna.

Among the writings of the Jewish tradition, we may mention, in addition to the "*Book of Jubilees*," transcribed in the community of the Essenes, the apocryphal "*Ascensio Mosis,*" *the* first part of which, properly called "*the Testament of Moses*," includes the prophetic farewell discourse addressed by Moses to his successor Joshua on Israel's future destiny and the end of time. It broadly describes the period of the Hasmoneans: a powerful king from the West will conquer the land, but Israel with God's help will succeed victoriously over Rome; then the final day will come. The text, written at the turn of the first century B.C. and the first century A.D., is also mentioned by the Church Fathers. The second, unpreserved part, "the *Ascension,*" *is* referred to in the New Testament letter of Jude, in the verses in which it recounts the episode where the archangel Michael wrestles with Satan to take possession of Moses' body.

In Philo of Alexandria's *De Vita* Mosis, Moses figures as a scholar of the Hellenistic period. He surpasses his Egyptian and Greek masters in knowledge and, as a shrewd man guided by reason, combines in himself the qualities of the philosopher and prophet with those of the king. According to Philo, Plato's doctrine on creation and Heraclitus' teaching on contraries also date back to him.

The Jewish historiographer Josephus Flavius writes a biography of Moses with admirable signs of his mission in his youth, ending with his rise to Egyptian viceroy. In his writing *Contra Apionem*, Moses is for Josephus Flavius the earliest lawgiver, and the laws of the Greeks also refer to him. According to Aristobulus of Alexandria, on the other hand, from the hand of Moses, Homer and Hesiod received the topics to be dealt with in their epic poems and dramas.

Christian Tradition

Christianity, born in the Jewish context and having in common with the Jews the Old Testament, sees in Moses the same characteristics of patriarch, lawgiver and leader of the Jewish people as in the Jewish tradition.The New Testament considers Moses above all as a prophet, who foretold the coming of Jesus as the Messiah, which is why he, along with Elijah, witnesses the transfiguration of Jesus

In addition to being an unheard witness of faith, as Stephen describes him in his extensive apologia Moses is also extolled in the letter to the Hebrews as an example of faith, as a servant of God not superior to Jesus who, according to Christianity, is God himself incarnate.

For the New Testament Moses is the lawgiver through whom God spoke, and thus he is the founder of the Old Testament salvific order. He is contrasted typologically with Jesus as the founder of the new order of salvation; in Moses and Jesus are contrasted the law of old on the one hand and the gospel on the other, the gospel understood as the perfection and not the demolition of the law itself.

In the following period Moses, also due to the influence of Jewish traditions, is considered a model of perfect life, of a constant ascent of the soul to God, so much so that the Christian tradition has reworked the life and figure of the biblical prophet from a Christological perspective, finding several concordances between his biography and that of Jesus Christ

Raymond Brown also believes that the narrative of Jesus' birth was modeled on that of Moses, itself derived from earlier traditions of other peoples. The scholar - with regard to the biblical narrative on the birth of Moses used by Matthew for the Nativity of Jesus - points out a number of parallels: Herod tries to kill Jesus and the latter is made to flee to another country; Pharaoh tries to kill Moses and the latter flees to another country; Herod orders the slaughter of the innocent (male children), Pharaoh that of the firstborn Hebrew males; Herod and Pharaoh both die while Jesus and Moses are in exile; an angel of the Lord warns Jesus' family that they can return to their land, and so does the Lord with Moses (in both cases Brown emphasizes the use of the same expression to justify returning to Israel (or Egypt): ""*because those who were undermining the child's life* (or: '*your life*') *died*"); Joseph takes wife and son and returns to Israel,

Moses takes wife and son and returns to Egypt. Brown points out that other sources on Moses' life - such as Flavius Josephus and various Jewish midrash - also "accentuate the already well-known biblical parallels between the childhoods of Moses and Jesus." To the same conclusions comes historian John Dominic Crossan, among the co-founders of the Jesus Seminar, who points out that, compared to the Lucan account, Matthew "instead of imagining barren couples and miraculous conceptions, focuses on Moses' childhood," creating the relevant parallels. Theologian Rudolf Bultmann also believes there are older, common traditions behind the narratives of the slaughter of the innocents commanded by Herod after the birth of Jesus and that of the slaughter of the Hebrew firstborn in the story of Moses.

He is venerated as a saint by the Catholic Church, which remembers him on September 4.

Islamic tradition

According to the Qur'ān Moses (*Mūsā*) was a great man, one of the major prophets predecessors of Muhammad as well as the prophet mentioned most frequently in the Qur'ān. He was rescued while still an infant from a persecution wished by Pharaoh (*Firawūn*), who feared the birth of a usurper, and adopted by the ruler's own wife (Āsija), who then entrusted the infant, by divine inspiration, to his birth mother to nurse him.

Growing up, one day he was confronted by two men, one Egyptian and one belonging to the Bani Israil. It should be specified that at the time the Bani Israil were victims of torture and were enslaved by Pharaoh, so Mūsā, killed the Egyptian and asked for forgiveness from Allah, who granted it to him.He fled to Midian and married the daughter (named Zippora?) of the man who had taken him into his tent, whom some scholars believe to be the messenger or prophet Shu'Ayb AS who at the time may have been there. He departed after concluding his appointed engagements and, passing with his people from Sinai, went off to look for an ember of fire and came near the holy valley Tuwa. There he was met by the voice of Allah, who ordered him to remove his shoes as he was in the holy valley and told him to throw his staff that he held in his right hand. This turned into a large snake, but taking it back it became a stick again as it was originally. Then, Allah told him to put his hand under his armpit and it became a bright light like the moon.Repeating the process, the hand returned to normal.This is why many times Muslims refer to Mūsā, as "Musa Kalimullah," meaning the one to whom Allah spoke directly.

He went to Pharaoh's presence and spoke to him very modestly so that he would free Bani Israil from constant oppression. But the latter did not want to hear anything. Mūsā and his brother Harun presented themselves to him as the Messengers of Allah, and Pharaoh wounded in his soul challenged him to a duel against his magicians on the feast day in Egypt. Mūsā threw his staff in front of the ruler's feet, and by the will of Allah alone, it turned into a serpent of a great size that no one had ever seen before, but so did the Egyptian magicians, making believe that they had brought some ropes to life, which were, however, very soon devoured by Mūsā's serpent. The enchanters, amazed by the prodigy, converted to the religion of Israel, being killed for it by Pharaoh. During the night Mūsā and Harun, on Allah's orders, left Egypt together with their people by crossing the sea and then closing in on the Egyptian army that had run after them.Pharaoh then realized that Allah's punishment, which Mūsā had long warned him about, had now begun and would come upon him and his accomplices if he did not repent of his actions and ask Allah for forgiveness; Pharaoh repented, but it was too late. He died as an unbeliever (kafir), along with his accomplices.

Upon ascending Sinai Mūsā left the command to Aaron (*Hārūn ibn Imrān*) who was overpowered by the people, particularly Samirī who built and worshipped a golden calf, and for this he was cast out by Mūsā and condemned to say, "Don't touch me," for the rest of his life. As they set out again for the desert, the Israelites complained to the prophet about the absence of water and food; he prayed to Allah, who rained down manna from the sky and gushed twelve springs from a rock. At that moment the tribes of Israel were born. Having come close to the Promised Land, because of their rebellion, the Israelites were punished with the forty years of exile in the desert.

Moses in art

The horns of Moses

Famous is the controversial debate that has arisen over the horns placed on Moses' head in various artistic works, such as Michelangelo's sculpture of the same name.

This iconological feature derives from the passage in Ex34:29, which in the original Hebrew text (Masoretic text) reports that, after receiving from God the tablets of the Ten Commandments, Moses was unaware that his skin was 'radiant' (Hebrew verb *qrn*). In written Hebrew, vowels are not inserted so that the same term can take on different meanings depending on the vowels the reader has chosen to insert or the meaning he or she has chosen to interpret. In this case, the triliteral root can denote either the term QARAN (also Karan), with the meaning of radiance in the sense of a luminous 'irradiation,' or the term QEREN (Keren), or 'horns' in the sense of the animal bony apparatus. The interpretation given by the Masoretes, which is the one preferred by the canonical religious community, is that the author intended to indicate precisely that Moses' face was luminous, radiating light.

When St. Jerome translated the Hebrew text into Latin in the Vulgate, the official version of the Bible for centuries in the Latin Church, he adopted this lesson, translating "ignorabat quod cornuta esset facies sua," that is, "he was unaware that his face was horned." This has been a source of inspiration for several artists for centuries, including the aforementioned Michelangelo Buonarroti.

As the study of the original languages of the Bible spread, the interpretation given by the Masoretes gradually took hold. Many painters, however, continued to prefer the traditional iconography of 'horned' Moses. In some cases, Moses' face was depicted with two beams of light, resembling horns, starting from the top of his head, a choice that connects the two interpretations at the same time.

Paintings

- (1475) *The Burning Bush*, by Nicolas Froment
- (1482) *Trials of Moses*, by Sandro Botticelli
- (1482) *Testament and Death of Moses*, by Luca Signorelli
- (1502-1505) Trial of Moses, by Giorgione.
- (1510) *Crossing the Red Sea*, by Bernardino Luini
- (1510-1512) Transfiguration, by Lorenzo Lotto
- (1523) *Moses and the Daughters of Jethro*, by Rosso Fiorentino
- (1525) *The water springing from the rock*, by Luke of Leiden

- (1537) *The Chastisement of Heavenly Fire*, by Domenico Beccafumi
- (1540) *The Crossing of the Red Sea*, by Lucas Cranach
- (1540-45) *Moses saved from the waters*, by Bonifacio de Pitati
- (1540-45) *Crossing the Red Sea*, by Agnolo Bronzino
- (1575) *Finding of Moses*, by Paolo Veronese
- (1577) *The Manna*, by Tintoretto
- (1577) *Moses brings forth water from the rock*, by Tintoretto
- (1609-10) *Moses defends the daughters of Jethro*, by Carlo Saraceni
- (1615) *The Manna*, by Guido Reni
- (1615) *Water sprung from the rock*, by Paolo Guidotti
- (1620) *The Bronze Serpent*, by Anton Van Dyck
- (1621) *The return of the explorers*, by Giovanni Lanfranco
- (1623) *The Burning Bush*, by Matteo Rosselli
- (1628-30) *Sacrifice of Moses*, by Massimo Stanzione
- (1630) *Moses saved from the waters*, by Orazio Gentileschi
- (1635) *The Golden Calf*, by Nicolas Poussin

- (1650) *Moses with the tables of the Law*, by Philippe de Champaigne
- (1654) *Moses entrusted to the waters*, by Nicolas Poussin
- (1659) *Moses breaks the tables of the Law*, by Rembrandt.
- (post 1808) *Moses with the tables of the law*, by Giuseppe Diotti
- (1904) *The Finding of Moses*, by Lawrence Alma-Tadema.
- (1950-1952) *Moses receives the tables of the law*, by Marc Chagall

Sculptures

- (1515) *Moses*, by Michelangelo Buonarroti

Literature

- Sigmund Freud, *The Man Moses and Monotheistic Religion* (*Der Mann Moses und die monotheistische Religion*) 1937-39, 3 essays. In the famous work, the father of psychoanalysis argues that Moses, an Egyptian by birth, had adhered to the monotheistic faith during the reign of Akhenaten (14th century BCE). When this was abolished with the death of the ruler and traditional Egyptian polytheism was restored, Moses 'converted' the Hebrews settled in Egyptian territory and pushed them toward

Palestine, the promised land of the God Aton-Adonai.

- Thomas Mann, *The Law* (original German title *Das Gesetz*), 1944. Moses is the bastard son of Pharaoh's daughter and a Hebrew servant. He feels called by God to liberate his people by clashing with Pharaoh Ramessu. The first nine plagues are natural events while the last one, the killing of the Egyptian firstborn, is carried out by the Hebrews. They flee in 12-13,000 through the Bitter Lakes, partially dried up by a strong wind.
- Christian Jacq, *Rameses* (1995-1997), 5 novels. Intercalated with the life of Pharaoh Rameses is the story of the Exodus. Moses, Rameses' Hebrew friend, integrated into Egyptian society, accepts Akhenaten's monotheism, now eradicated from Egypt. Becoming a fanatical visionary, he incites the Jews, working but not enslaved, against Pharaoh and the Egyptians. He implements and orders a number of tricks and deceptions to generate the plagues, eventually driving the Hebrews unwillingly out of Egypt.

Music

Moses appears in Gioachino Rossini's opera Moses in
Egypt of 1818 and its French remake Moïse et Pharaon,
ou Le Passage de la mer Rouge of 1827, as well as in the
opera *Moses und Aron* composed by Arnold Schoenberg
between 1930 and 1932. He also stars in numerous
oratorios, including those by Giovanni Paolo Colonna,
Vincenzo de Grandis, Adolf Bernhard Marx, Max Bruch,
Lorenzo Perosi and Marco Frisina.

Other books by United Library

https://campsite.bio/unitedlibrary